W9-DAA-029

MISS MOPP'S LUCKY DAY

To librarians, parents, and teachers:

Miss Mopp's Lucky Day is a Parents Magazine READ ALOUD Original — one title in a series of colorfully illustrated and fun-to-read stories that young readers will be sure to come back to time and time again.

Now, in this special school and library edition of *Miss Mopp's Lucky Day*, adults have an even greater opportunity to increase children's responsiveness to reading and learning — and to have fun every step of the way.

When you finish this story, check the special section at the back of the book. There you will find games, projects, things to talk about, and other educational activities designed to make reading enjoyable by giving children and adults a chance to play together, work together, and talk over the story they have just read.

For a free color catalog describing Gareth Stevens' list of high-quality books, call 1-800-542-2595 (USA) or 1-800-461-9120 (Canada). Gareth Stevens' Fax (414) 225-0377.

Parents Magazine READ ALOUD Originals:

A Garden for Miss Mouse
Aren't You Forgetting
    Something, Fiona?
Bicycle Bear
The Biggest Shadow in
    the Zoo
Bread and Honey
Buggly Bear's Hiccup Cure
But No Elephants
Cats! Cats! Cats!
The Clown-Arounds
The Clown-Arounds Go
    on Vacation
Elephant Goes to School
The Fox with Cold Feet
Get Well, Clown-Arounds!
The Ghost in Dobbs Diner
The Giggle Book
The Goat Parade
Golly Gump Swallowed a Fly
Henry Babysits

Henry Goes West
Henry's Awful Mistake
Henry's Important Date
The Housekeeper's Dog
The Little Witch Sisters
The Man Who Cooked
    for Himself
Milk and Cookies
Miss Mopp's Lucky Day
No Carrots for Harry!
Oh, So Silly!
The Old Man and the
    Afternoon Cat
One Little Monkey
The Peace-and-Quiet Diner
Pets I Wouldn't Pick
Pickle Things
Pigs in the House
Rabbit's New Rug
Rupert, Polly, and Daisy
Sand Cake

Septimus Bean and His
    Amazing Machine
Sheldon's Lunch
Sherlock Chick and the
    Giant Egg Mystery
Sherlock Chick's First Case
The Silly Tail Book
Snow Lion
Socks for Supper
Sweet Dreams, Clown-
    Arounds!
Ten Furry Monsters
There's No Place Like Home
This Farm is a Mess
Those Terrible Toy-Breakers
Up Goes Mr. Downs
The Very Bumpy Bus Ride
Where's Rufus?
Who Put the Pepper in
    the Pot?
Witches Four

Library of Congress Cataloging-in-Publication Data

McGuire, Leslie.
    Miss Mopp's lucky day / by Leslie McGuire; pictures by Jody Silver.
        p. cm. -- (Parents magazine read aloud original)
    "North American library edition"--T.p. verso.
    Summary: While walking through the woods to deliver her cakes,
the unobservant Miss Mopp avoids disaster when the threat of rain
makes her remember something she forgot.
    ISBN 0-8368-0992-0
    [1. Luck--Fiction. 2. Humorous stories.] I. Silver, Jody, ill.
II. Title. III. Series.
PZ7.M4786Mi 1994
[E]--dc20   94-11309

This North American library edition published in 1994 by Gareth Stevens Publishing, 1555 North RiverCenter Drive, Suite 201, Milwaukee, Wisconsin, 53212, USA, under an arrangement with Pages, Inc., St. Petersburg, Florida.

Text © 1981 by Leslie McGuire. Illustrations © 1981 by Jody Silver. End matter © 1994 by Gareth Stevens, Inc.

All rights reserved. No part of this book may be reproduced or used in any form or by any means without permission in writing from the publisher.

Printed in the United States of America

1 2 3 4 5 6 7 8 9 99 98 97 96 95 94

Miss Mopp's Lucky Day

A Parents Magazine
Read Aloud Original

Miss Mopp's Lucky Day

By LESLIE McGUIRE Pictures by JODY SILVER

Parents Magazine Press • New York
Gareth Stevens Publishing • Milwaukee

É MeG

To David: May all your days be lucky – L.M.

To my daughter, Leigh – J.S.

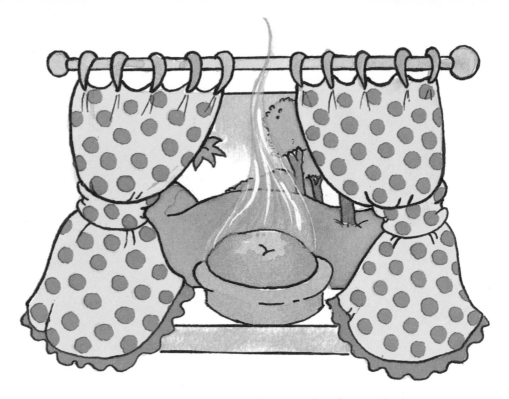

Miss Mopp was the best baker in town.
She baked all kinds of cakes —
pink cakes and yellow cakes,
big cakes and small cakes,
plain cakes and fancy cakes.

One morning Miss Mopp
woke up and said,
"Today is my lucky day!
I just know I will sell
all my cakes."

13

So, as soon as she finished her baking,
Miss Mopp got dressed and
carefully wrapped her cakes
to take to town.

15

Just as she stepped outside,
the sun went behind a cloud.
It was a big, gray rain cloud.
But Miss Mopp did not see it.

She went a few steps, then stopped.
"Did I forget something?"
she asked herself.
"Oh well, I can't think what it might be."
And on she went.

As she walked, the smell of
the delicious cakes went before her.
It was a very good smell.

Now, deep in the woods,
smelling that smell,
was a bear.
"Mmm," said the bear.
"Miss Mopp's cakes.
I want to gobble them up!"
And the bear hid behind a tree.

The bear was not the only one
smelling the smell of Miss Mopp's cakes.
There was also a moose.
"Mmm," said the moose.
"Miss Mopp's cakes.
I want to gobble them up!"
So the moose hid
on the other side of the tree.

Miss Mopp walked along happily.
She did not see that up in the tree,
smelling the smell of her delicious cakes,
there was a bird.
"Mmm," said the bird.
"Miss Mopp's cakes.
I want to gobble them up!"
And the bird hid behind a big leaf.

The sky was getting
darker and darker.
Miss Mopp tried to remember
what she had forgotten.
She still did not see
the big, gray rain cloud.

And she did not see the fat raccoon
and the furry rabbit.
They were smelling the smell
of the delicious cakes, too.
"Mmm," they each said.
"Miss Mopp's cakes.
I want to gobble them up!"
And they hid in two hollows in the tree.

Then, just as the bear, the moose,
the bird, the raccoon, and the rabbit
were about to jump out
to gobble up the cakes,
Miss Mopp stopped and yelled...

"MY UMBRELLA!
I forgot my UMBRELLA!"
And she ran back to her house while...

The rabbit dashed out
  and hit the raccoon
    who tripped the bear
      who fell on the moose
        who got hit on the head by the bird.

Miss Mopp made it back to her house
just before the rain began.
She picked up her umbrella
and started off again.

She walked through the woods,
past the tree, and into town,
without meeting anyone at all.

When she got to the bake shop
she saw a line outside.
"My stars!" said Miss Mopp.
"Look at all
those customers
waiting to buy
my cakes.
This is truly
my lucky day!"

But Miss Mopp
didn't know how lucky
she really was, did she?

Notes to Grown-ups

Major Themes

Here is a quick guide to the significant themes and concepts at work in *Miss Mopp's Lucky Day*:

- Improperly acquiring something you desire leads to trouble.
- Joining a group whose members set a bad example has its consequences.

Step-by-step Ideas for Reading and Talking

Here are some ideas for further give-and-take between grown-ups and children. The following topics encourage creative discussion of *Miss Mopp's Lucky Day* and invite the kind of open-ended response that is consistent with many contemporary approaches to reading, including Whole Language:

- Has your child ever wanted something so badly that he or she was willing to steal for it? Explain to your child why stealing is wrong and how it can lead to much more trouble than it is worth.
- Explain to your child the importance of having self esteem. Explain that when a person does something to take advantage of another person or a situation, it erodes the self esteem of the person taking advantage.
- Miss Mopp is lucky in more ways than one. How many ways can you and your child think of to show how lucky Miss Mopp is? For example: She is lucky to have a job she enjoys. She is lucky to have the talent to do the job. She is lucky to have a cat. She is lucky that her cakes did not get wet. She is lucky to have made it through the woods safely, etc. In what ways is your child lucky?

Games for Learning

Games and activities can stimulate young readers and listeners alike to find out more about words, numbers, and ideas. Here are more ideas for turning learning into fun:

Lucky-Clover Cake

Ask your child to think of some things that are supposed to bring good luck. Your child might include a four-leaf clover in his or her list of lucky charms. See if your child can think of any places where he or she has seen a four-leaf clover (for example, on cereal boxes or St. Patrick's Day decorations). Then you and your child can make a "lucky-clover cake" following the directions below.

Prepare and bake a round cake following the directions on a box of chocolate cake mix. Let the cake cool and then carefully remove it from the pan. Cut the cake into quarters and then shape each section with a knife so that it resembles a leaf of a four-leaf clover. Save one "shaving" of cake to be used as a stem for your lucky cake. Position the four pieces and stem so they resemble a four-leaf clover. Add several drops of green food coloring to canned white frosting and then ice the leaves of the cake. With any luck at all, you and your child will have a delicious cake to share!

Who Nose?

The animals in the woods could smell Miss Mopp's delicious cakes as she carried them toward the shop in town. Talk with your child about the sense of smell and explain why it is important to people and animals. Then play a game of "Who Nose?" Put small amounts of common and easily recognizable foods (for example, peanut butter, lemon juice) in small containers. Conceal the contents of the containers or have your child close his or her eyes. Can your child identify the foods using the sense of smell only?

44

About the Author

LESLIE McGUIRE believes people are lucky if they *think* they are lucky. For example, if Miss Mopp was feeling gloomy, she might have said, "My stars, what a dreadful day! I forgot my umbrella, I had to run back home for it, then it rained, and my cakes were almost ruined!" "So you see," explains Ms. McGuire, "it's all in how you look at it!"

Ms. McGuire was a teacher and a children's book editor before she turned to writing children's books full time. Her first book for Parents, which she wrote and illustrated, was *This Farm is a Mess*.

Ms. McGuire lives in New York City with her husband and their son. She thinks they have lots of lucky days. "I hope all *your* days are lucky, too!" she says.

About the Artist

JODY SILVER says she liked Miss Mopp immediately, even though she and Miss Mopp don't have much in common. "For example, I can't cook at all," she says. "Even my two cats don't like my cooking. I think they prefer Purina!"

Ms. Silver writes and illustrates children's books, and she is also an animator. An animator is a person who draws the pictures for cartoons, like the ones you see on television. Ms. Silver has animated cartoons for *Sesame Street*, and she has made two animated films of her own. *Miss Mopp's Lucky Day* is the first book she has illustrated for Parents.

Ms. Silver lives in New York City with her husband and their daughter.

McGuire, Leslie.
Miss Mopp's lucky day
E McG

000010390490

DATE DUE

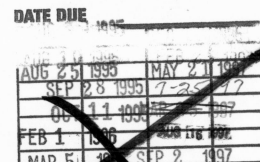

AUG 25 1995	MAY 21 199
SEP 28 1995	7-25-97
OCT 11 1995	997
FEB 1 1996	AUG 118 1997
MAR 5 199	SEP 2 1997
MAY 4 1996	SEP 24 1997
AUG 1996	OCT 8 1997
OCT 8 1996	MAY 26 1998
2001	JUL 1 3 1998

RAL ✓ 09920

951154

E
McG McGuire, Leslie
Miss Mopp's lucky day